COLORING BOOK

FARM ANIMALS

THIS BOOK BELONGS TO:

_____

_____

FARM ANIMALS

DOG

GOOSE

CAT

PEACOCK

HEN

DUCK

TURKEY

OSTRICH

FARM ANIMALS

RABBIT

GOAT

PIG

HORSE

COW

ALPACA

SHEEP

DONKEY

DID YOU KNOW?
A dog's baby is called a puppy.

Fun facts: Dogs were the first animal domesticated (tamed) by humans, over 20,000 years ago! As they evolved from wolves, their skulls, teeth and paws shrank, and they became more docile and obedient.

DID YOU KNOW?
A cat's baby is called a kitten.

Fun facts: A house cat is genetically 95.6% tiger. Cats walk like camels and giraffes, both right feet then both left feet. Also, cats can jump 5 times their height.

DID YOU KNOW?
A hen's baby is called a chick.

Fun facts: The chicken is the closest living relative to the T-Rex. Chickens have over 200 distinct noises they can make for communicating.

Fun facts: The color of the shell depends on the breed of the hen that laid it. The color of the yolk depends on the hen's diet. A dark yellow yolk means the hen ate vegetables, and a lighter yolk indicates a diet of wheat and barley.

DID YOU KNOW? A duck's baby is called a duckling.

Fun facts: Ducklings are born ready to leave the nest within hours of hatching - their eyes are open and they are able to find some of their own food. Ducks' feathers are waterproof.

DID YOU KNOW?
A turkey's baby is called a poult.

Fun facts: Turkeys can change colors. You can tell a turkey's emotions by the color of their heads. Colors can change from red to blue to white, depending on how excited or calm they are. The more intense the colors are, the more intense their emotions.

Fun facts: Geese preening their feathers, foraging for food in the grass, and collecting twigs, bark, and leaves to use to make "home improvements" in their nests. Geese are faithful, mate for life, and mourn when their partner dies.

DID YOU KNOW?
A peacock's baby is called a peachick.

Fun facts: Peacocks are omnivores, feeding on insects, plants, and small animals. Only the male peafowls have eye-catching color and lovely decorative tail feathers.

DID YOU KNOW?

Ostrich's baby is called a chick or a hatchling.

Fun facts: Ostriches are the largest and heaviest birds on Earth and they produce the world's biggest eggs. Ostriches can't fly but they run really fast and contrary to popular belief, ostriches do not bury their heads in the sand.

DID YOU KNOW?
A rabbit's baby is called a bunny.

Fun facts: A rabbit's teeth never stop growing! Instead, they're gradually worn down as the rabbit chews on grasses, wildflowers and vegetables – meaning they never get too long. Carrots aren't a natural part of a rabbit's diet and can give bunnies an upset stomach if they eat too many.

DID YOU KNOW? A pig's baby is called a piglet.

Fun facts: Pigs are considered the 4th most intelligent animal (after chimpanzees, dolphins, and elephants). Pigs don't have sweat glands, so they must roll in mud to stay cool and prevent sunburns.

DID YOU KNOW?
A cow's baby is called a calf.

Fun facts: Cows are social animals who form bonds with each other. In a herd of cows, many will form cliques together. Cows can sense a storm coming and will lie down. Cows have a memory of about three years.

Fun facts: Sheep make a bleating sound. A baby lamb can identify its mother by her bleat. Sheep have two toes on each foot.

DID YOU KNOW?
A goat's baby is called a kid.

Fun facts: The goat is among the cleanest of animals, and is a much more selective feeder than cows, sheep, pigs, chickens and even dogs. Goats do eat many different species of plants, but don't want to eat food that has been contaminated or that has been on the floor or the ground.

Fun facts: Horses can't breathe through their mouth, only through their nose. Horses can sleep standing up. On average, they sleep two and a half hours per day. Foals can walk and run within a few hours after birth.

DID YOU KNOW?
An alpaca's baby is called a cria.

Fun facts: Alpacas are herd animals and don't like to be alone. When their own kind aren't around, they like to live with llamas, goats, and sheep but always want the company of their own kind.

Fun facts: Donkeys can act as guard animals for livestock. They can defend against a dog, coyote, fox, or even bobcat that's bothering a herd of sheep or goats. Donkeys' large ears help them stay cool.

A FARM

A Gift for You!

Hey, dear parents, here's a Free Gift for your kid!

As a way of saying thank you for buying this book, I am offering a FREE printable Gift: "5 Farm Animals Activities to Train Kids' Attention and Skills". It's a fun and screen-free activity for your kid!

Just SCAN the code to get it!

(Open the camera on your phone as if you're going to take a photo, hold the phone over the QR code below, then a link will appear on your screen. Tap on the link to get your free download!)

Enjoy!

Thank You!

As the author of this Coloring Book, I wanted to take a moment to express our heartfelt gratitude for choosing our book and completing this incredible journey. It brings us great joy to know that our small, family-owned company has been a part of your life.

At our company, we pour our hearts and souls into creating quality children's books that inspire and empower young minds, just like you.

If you enjoyed this journal and found it to be a source of joy, encouragement, and growth, we kindly invite you to leave a review on Amazon. Your words carry immense power and can make a significant impact on our small business. Your support will not only help us reach more children but also inspire us to continue creating meaningful books.

We understand that leaving a review may seem like a small action, but to us, it means the world. Your support will enable us to continue producing quality books that touch the lives of young readers and nourish their imaginations.

With gratitude,
Cathleen Duncan

Contact us!

It is important for us to let you know that we appreciate any feedback on our creations and if you have any suggestions for improvement, you can contact us at our email address:

✉️

cathleenduncan.books@gmail.com

———— · —— — ————

Are you following us on Pinterest?

Ⓟ

If not, down below you can find the link to our Pinterest page, where you can see other creations we have made, announcements about our books or announcements about our new releases.

pinterest.com/cathleenduncanbooks/

With deep appreciation,
Cathleen Duncan